GOD'S PLAN FOR LOVE

LGBTQIA2S+: HOW DID WE GET HERE?

DR. TITILOLA NWAFOR

GOD'S PLAN FOR LOVE

WRITTEN BY

DR. TITILOLA NWAFOR

nwafortitilola@gmail.com

Published by:

COMMUNE WRITERS INT'L

www.communewriters.com

communewriterspublishing@gmail.com

+234 8139 260 389

6, Amusa Street, Agodo-Egbe, Lagos

Published in the Federal Republic of Nigeria

CONTENTS

A kid-friendly handbook for young Christians to help them understand the concept of LGBTQ+ and to guide them against it.

INTRODUCTION

Welcome, darling! You are about to explore something you have probably not heard of before in a much more fun, interesting, engaging and yet biblical way!

Common, tell me, have you heard of LGBTQIA2S+ before? Doesn't it look to you like letters arranged in a disordered manner?

What if I told you that each letter stands for something special?

You see, the very first time I heard it, it sounded like a kind of password to unlock a device and I was very curious to find out what it actually meant just like you are curious now.

Somehow, it took me a while to fully understand the meaning of the initials. But you know what? This is not going to be your case because, in this beautiful book in your hands, you will learn what LGBTQIA2S+ is in the simplest form ever.

Not just that, you will understand why you should know about it even as a kid, the origin and motive behind it, what the bible says about it, and if it is what you should embrace as a child of God.

Oh, I know you cannot wait to get in. Kindly adjust your curiosity caps, grab a bowl of your favourite ice cream and get ready for an extraordinary adventure!

Are you ready? Great! Let us turn the page and begin our adventure!

See you on the other side!

CHAPTER ONE

WHAT IS LGBTQIA2S+?

I am so happy for you darling. In a few minutes, you are about to find out what took some people several years to discover.

As I had earlier said in the introduction of this book, LGBTQIA2S+ is an initiative that represents a particular set of people whose gender identity defer from the usual ones. The LGBTQIA2S+ people belong to a community which is also known as the Rainbow Community. Do not worry, I will talk more about this later in this book.

So quickly, let us look at what these scattered letters mean. One by one, I will be picking and explaining each and I want you to follow me along. Are we good?

The first letter is L.

L stands for **Lesbian**.

Lesbian is a word used to describe two girls or women who are sexually attracted to each other. You don't seem to understand that, right? Ok, let me put it in simpler terms. You see, a girl or woman who marries a fellow girl or woman is called a Lesbian and the act is called Lesbianism. Do you understand it now?

Good! Let's move on to the next letter which is letter G.

G stands for **Gay.**

Gay has the same definition as Lesbian just that in this case, it is about men/boys and not women or girls. This best describes two boys or men that are sexually attracted to each other.

The next letter is B.

B stands for **Bisexual**.

You must have heard about this, before. Haven't you? Well, bisexual is simply a term used to describe someone who is sexually attracted to both men and women.

What letter do we have next?

Letter T, right?

Ok. **T** stands for **Transgender**.

Now, this might seem a bit tricky but trust me, I will do my best to break it down. Okay?

A Transgender is someone who behaves differently from his or her sex. I will explain, don't worry.

It means that they feel like they are not the gender they were assigned at birth. For example, a person assigned female at birth might feel that they are a boy instead. And a person assigned male at birth might feel deep that they are a girl instead.

Do you get it?

Fine, let us move to the next letter which is Q.

Q stands for **Queer**.

Queer is a word used to describe someone who does not know where they belong. Sometimes, it is used as a general term to classify people who belong to the LGBTQIA2S+ community.

It is used for people who find it hard to place themselves in any categories or if they are still trying to figure out how they feel. Sometimes, they are referred to as gay.

Is it clear?

Alright then, let's keep moving! The next letter is I.

I stand for **Intersex**.

Intersex is used for describing someone who has physical and biological characteristics that do not present them as male (boys or men) or female (girls or women). They cannot tell if they are male or female.

I think this one is quite simple to grasp.

Hurriedly, let us move on to the next letter which is A.

A stands for **Asexual**.

Asexual is a word that describes someone who is not sexually attracted to anyone. They are neither attracted to boys nor are they attracted to girls. Is this clear enough?

Good! We are almost done. Now, let us move on to the next which is 2S

2S stands for **Two Spirit.**

Sarah Hunt defines it as a way by which Indigenous people identify someone who has both female and male spirits. Two-Spirit is used to describe people who have both male and female qualities. They have both boys' and girls' features.

Two-spirit is the native word for identities that are recognized at different localities. It means different things in each nation and to each person who holds that identity.

It is almost like a local language spoken by particular people that cannot be used or known by others. Each community has its words which best describe their identities.

I really do hope you understand this.

Finally, let's look at the last symbol which is **+**

The symbol **+** is not the regular Mathematics addition sign you know. Here, it is used to represent other gender identities that are not written here. There are so many of them that are yet to be identified.

Yes! That is all we will be having for this chapter. Now, you know that LGBTQIA2S+ is not a kind of scattered letter but an initial that represents a particular set of people. We always have this kind of people around us: both in school, churches and homes. However, we must learn to respect and love everyone, especially as a child of God. Do you get that?

Good! Turn over to the next chapter and let us look at how this LGBTQIA2S+ Community started.

Hope you are still with your bowl of ice cream.☺

CHAPTER TWO

THE ORIGIN

Hello friend. Here, I am going to tell a story of how LGBTQIA2S+ started. And I will still go further to tell you about their movement across the world and their mission. Are you ready to do this with me?

Beautiful! Common, let us dive in to discover how this community came to be!

Once upon a time, in a world not too different from ours, there was a diverse group of people called the LGBTQIA2S+ community. Then, people did not have the same understanding of different sexual identities as we do now. But they still lived lives similar to what we now call LGBTQ. It was not until the middle of the 1900s that the idea of being gay became clear. Back then, the words they used to talk about sexuality and gender were not as specific as they are today.

One British scientist, Havelock Ellis, called people who were attracted to the same gender or didn't fit traditional gender roles "sexual inverts." He meant that they were different from what was expected based on their birth sex. Another scholar, Karl Ulrichs from Germany, used the term "Urning" to describe a third gender that existed between men and women. These words were used to describe people we might now call gay, transgender, or genderqueer. Ulrichs believed that male Urnings had the hearts of women in male bodies, and female Urnings had the hearts of men in female bodies.

The word "homosexual" which means sexual relationship between two people that are of the same gender was first used in 1869, but it didn't become popular until later. In the middle of the 1900s, some people who were fighting for the rights of gay people preferred to use the word "homophile" because it sounded less focused on sex and more accepting of same-gender attraction.

The word "gay" started being used in secret during the early 1900s and became more common in the 1960s. The people from the Stonewall generation, who came after the earlier activists, felt less ashamed and saw being gay as a normal part of life, not something to be hidden. They wanted to make a stronger statement and distance themselves from the more moderate homophile groups.

Back then, the word "gay" was used to describe everyone in the LGBTQ community, not just gay men. For example, Sylvia Rivera and Marsha P. Johnson, who were transgender women of colour, used "gay rights" and "gay power" to fight for their rights and help homeless transgender youth. They started an organization called STAR to support people who were struggling at that time.

So, over time, people have used different words to describe and understand different sexual identities, and these words have changed and evolved. Today, we use a variety of terms like gay, lesbian, bisexual, transgender, and more to recognize the diversity of people's identities and experiences.

CHAPTER THREE

THE MOVEMENT OF THE LGBTQIA2S+ COMMUNITY

Hey friend! Let us talk about the LGBTQ+ community and their fight for equal rights in Africa. It is a bit complicated, but I will make it simple for you!

The LGBTQ+ community includes people who are lesbian, gay, bisexual, transgender, queer and others who identify as a sexual or gender minority.

Different parts of the world have different stories when it comes to LGBTQ+ rights.

Let us take a quick trip around the globe and see what is happening in each region:

North America:

In the United States, there have been some great movements! Same-sex marriage became legal nationwide in 2015, and many states have passed laws to protect LGBTQ+ people from discrimination. However, there are still important issues to address, especially when it comes to transgender rights and making sure everyone has access to healthcare and public facilities.

Canada has also made great progress. They legalized same-sex marriage in 2005 and have put laws in place to protect LGBTQ+ people. They are still working on issues like transgender rights, conversion therapy bans, and making sure everyone is treated fairly no matter their background.

Europe:

Many countries in Europe have made big strides in LGBTQ+ rights. In countries like the Netherlands, Belgium, and Germany, same-sex marriage is legal! They're also working on protecting transgender rights and making sure everyone is treated equally, no matter their gender identity. However, there are still some challenges in Eastern European countries where LGBTQ+ individuals face discrimination and have fewer legal protections.

Latin America:

In Latin America, Argentina and Uruguay were the first countries in the region to make same-sex marriage legal. Many other countries have also passed laws to protect LGBTQ+ people from discrimination. But there are violence and discrimination against LGBTQ+ individuals, especially transgender people in some areas.

Africa:

In Africa, there are challenges for the LGBTQ+ movement. Some countries in Africa have laws that make homosexuality illegal, and people who identify as LGBTQ+ can face legal troubles because of it. However, South Africa recognizes same-sex marriage and has laws to protect LGBTQ+ rights. In 2006, they even made it legal for same-sex couples to get married.

But things are different in other parts of Africa. LGBTQ+ rights are not widely accepted and face many challenges. Some African countries have laws that make it illegal to be gay.

However, even in these tough situations, some people are agitating that they make LGTBQ+ legal in all African countries.

Asia:

LGBTQ+ rights in Asia are different from country to country. Some countries, like Taiwan, have taken steps forward by legalizing same-sex marriage. But in some Asian nations, being gay or lesbian is still considered a crime, and LGBTQ+ individuals face discrimination and limited legal protections.

Australia:

In Australia, they had a national referendum in 2017, and as a result, same-sex marriage became legal! They are also making progress in other LGBTQ+ rights, like anti-discrimination laws. They are still addressing issues such as transgender rights, conversion therapy, and making sure everyone has access to good healthcare. In other Pacific Island nations, LGBTQ+ rights are still evolving, and some people are still working to promote acceptance and legal recognition.

The LGBTQ+ movement is a diverse and complex struggle for equality and acceptance worldwide. While these movements have been widely accepted in some regions, there are still some countries that strictly tag it as illegal.

Now, you know the origin of the LGBTQIA2S+ Community and their movement across the world.

Hope your ice cream is still very cold because we still have a lot of journey to cover.☺

The next we will be doing is to find out what God has to say concerning these people. You know what? I am so excited because this adventure is getting more interesting. Are you excited too?

Great! Let us go!

<u>CHAPTER FOUR</u>

WHAT DID GOD SAY ABOUT LGBTQIA2S+ PEOPLE?

Hi darling! I know you are eager to know what God says about these peculiar people. You want to know if it was God who created these LGBTQIA2S+ people. If God was the one, why did He decide to create them that way?

Wait, do you have your Holy Bible with you there? Quickly get it now because we are going to be reading through the Bible together.

In the Beginning...

If we want to know everything that God has to say about LGBTQ+ Community, we have to start from the beginning of the Bible. This is why we will be reading from the first book of the Bible which is Genesis.

So, kindly turn over to the book of Genesis chapter 1 and let us read from verse 1 and we will jump over to verse 27. I will read from my Bible here. It says,

"In the beginning, God created the heaven and the earth"

Verse 27: ***"So God created man in his image, in the image of God created he him; male and female created he them."***

Is your Bible saying the same thing as mine? Ok, let's discuss what the Bible just said.

In this account of creation, we learnt that in the very beginning, God made heaven and earth including everything in them. And it was specifically stated that God made man in His image and as a Male (Boy/Man) and Female (Girl/Woman).

You can see, it is not written that God made some to be both man and woman in one body. No! God did not mix the two. Rather, God made man to be a man and a woman to be a woman.

But did you know that God created a woman from a man? Yes, He did! If you ever doubt me, turn your Bible to chapter 2 of Genesis and read verses 21 and 22.

Did you see what happened there? God made Adam (a man) to sleep very deeply and God quietly and gently removed one of Adam's bones (ribs) and He used it to make Eve (a woman). This is one of the reasons why both man and woman have some features in common, although there are more to this scientifically.

For example, both men and women have eyes, noses, ears, hands, legs, and so on. But there are parts of the body that are specific to men alone and women alone. These parts make a man a man and a woman a woman.

You can see that God never had it in His plans that a man should marry a man or a man should marry a woman. If He wanted it to be like that He would have created man for Adam instead of a woman. God's only plan is that a man should marry a woman and a woman should marry a man.

Now, you may want to ask, "Since God did not create man to behave like a woman or woman to behave like a man, why then do we have people who are identified as LGBTQIA2S+?"

Hmm, you have just asked a brilliant question and as a matter of fact, scientists are still figuring out all the cool details.

You see, our bodies are like a fantastic mix of ingredients. Just like a recipe for cookies needs different things like flour, sugar, and butter, our bodies have special ingredients too. Some of these ingredients come from our genes, which are like tiny instructions inside us.

Now, when it comes to being LGBTQ+, these genes might play a part, but it is not as simple as having one special "LGBTQ+ gene." It is more like a big recipe with many genes, each adding a little touch to who we are.

But genes are not the only factors at play here. Our bodies go through some exciting changes before we are even born! It is like a magical transformation. These changes happen because of hormones, which are like little messengers in our bodies. They can influence how we grow and develop.

Sometimes, the levels of these hormones while we are growing inside our mom's belly can affect our feelings of being attracted to boys, girls, or both, and how we feel about our gender.

But guess what? Our surroundings and experiences also shape who we are! Just like friends and family can influence the games we like to play or the music we enjoy, they can also influence our feelings about love and our own identity.

Some people are living as LGBTQ+ today because they saw one either on TV shows, in their schools, worship centres, homes or neighbourhood.

Different cultures and societies have different ideas about love and gender, and that can make a big difference in how people see themselves. Some places celebrate and accept all kinds of love, while others don't.

In summary, the cause of people living as LGBTQ+ could be a result of hormonal changes within their bodies or environmental impacts.

Okay, I have been able to answer your question but I have a question for you too.

Now that you know that it is not in God's will for people to live as LGBTQIA2S+, do you think it is good for a child of God to live as one?

I will provide you with tips to rightfully answer this question. In the book of Leviticus 18:22 and Leviticus 20:13, God said it is a sin to practice gay or lesbianism and that His people should not involve in it.

Also, in the book of Romans 1:26-27, Apostle Paul spoke against men marrying men (Gay) and women marrying women (Lesbians). It is a great sin before God.

Okay, let me read verse 22 and 24 of Leviticus chapter 18.

Verse 22 (NIV) says, "Do not have sexual relations with a man as one does with a woman; that is detestable."

What does the above verse mean? It means as a man, you must not have sexual act with a fellow man and as a woman, you must not have sexual act with a fellow woman. Then in verse 24, God said something that I will like us to discuss.

Verse 24 (KJV): "Defile not ye yourselves in any of these things: for in all these the nations are defiled which I cast out before you"

This means God has destroyed a country where people practiced gay and lesbianism before. Now, let's find out the name of the country and how God destroyed them. Turn your Bible with me to the book of Genesis 19:1–24. Because the bible passage is lengthy, I will simply bring out our main points.

According to the passage, God destroyed the cities of Sodom and Gomorrah for their various sinful practices which includes gay. This was confirmed when two angels who were men visited the land and the men of Sodom and Gomorrah wanted to have sexual act with the angels. This got God very angry and He did something terrible in verse 24. Let's read it together.

Verse 24 (KJV) says, "Then the Lord rained upon Sodom and upon Gomorrah brimstone and fire from the Lord out of heaven"

What! God destroyed the two cities with rain of fire. The whole country caught fire and everyone and everything in it got burnt completely. This is how hard God can be on anyone who practices gay or lesbianism.

Even till today, God has reserved great fire for anyone who will not repent from committing sin.

Now, at this point, I need to clarify something very important. There is a big difference between someone who behaves like the opposite gender and someone who practices gay or lesbianism.

A boy can have a natural voice that sounds like that of a girl or walking steps that look like that of a girl, this does not make the boy gay or belong to the LGBTQ+ community. He only becomes gay when he is performing sexual acts with a fellow boy or when he marries a man. He only becomes a transgender if he decides to change his complete appearance and gender to a girl by going through some medical processes and wearing makeups.

So, when you see a boy who looks and does things like a girl or a girl who looks and does things like a boy, do not be too quick to assume that they belong to the LGBTQ+ community.

Back to my question,

"Is it a sin for a child of God to be identified as a member of the LGBTQ IA2S+ community?"

Yes, it is a sin for a child of God to belong to the LGBTQIA2S+ community. This is because, in this community, people of the same gender marry each other and have sexual acts with each other which is totally against the rules and plans of God.

My dear, do not let anybody deceive you into changing your gender. Those people who transitioned, especially the ones who went through some medical processes to change their gender are living in severe pain. Be always happy for who you are.

That will be all for now.

Did you remember that I told you in chapter 1 of this book that the LGBTQIA2S+ community is also known as Rainbow Community? It is time to look into the origin of the Rainbow in the Bible and why the LGBTQ+ community decided to use the Rainbow as their symbol. Common, show some excitement!

Let us go there!

CHAPTER FIVE

BEAUTIFUL RAINBOW

Back then as a kid, I was always excited anytime the rainbow appeared in the sky and I am sure you do the same as a kid. You know what a rainbow is, right? It is those colourful arches that appear in the sky after it rains.

Your Sunday school teacher must have told you about the ugly story behind the beautiful rainbow in the Bible. I hope you still have your Bible with you. Quickly open the book of Genesis 9:11-17 and if you want to read the full story, begin your reading from chapter 6 to chapter 9.

It is alright, I know that is quite lengthy I will do my best to summarize the whole story for you. Back then, during the time of a man called Noah, the people of the earth were very wicked and did all manner of things that made God got very angry that He decided to wipe out the entire earth including all the animals with heavy rain.

But Noah was a good man who feared and obeyed God. So, God spoke to Noah of His intention to destroy the whole earth and instructed Noah to build a very big ark which looked like a big ship. He also commanded Noah to take some of the animals inside and all of his family members.

Noah did all that God asked him to do and as soon as the rain started, Noah and his family members entered the big ark and God locked the ark by Himself.

Just as God has said, it rained heavily for forty days and by this time, the whole earth was covered with water. That was how God wiped all the wicked people and every other from the earth.

Finally, when the water dried up, Noah, his entire family and the animals all came out to offer the sacrifice of thanks to God who kept their lives.

Then, God promised never to destroy the earth with water again and He gave the rainbow as a sign of His promise.

So, that is why a rainbow always appears after heavy rain. Rainbow appears after heavy rainfall to remind us of God's promise that God will not destroy the earth with water again.

That is all about the story. But the question is **why did the LGBTQ+ community choose the Rainbow to be their symbol?**

Here is the short story, friend.

A long time ago, the people of the LGBTQ+ community wanted to have a special symbol to show who they were and that they were proud of themselves. They wanted something that would represent all the different kinds of people in their community.

So, an artist named Gilbert Baker came up with the idea of using a rainbow as their symbol which he did by making a rainbow flag.

The LGBTQ+ community loved the rainbow flag because it showed that they were all different, just like the colours of the rainbow, yet they were unique and united. And that is what they use up to date as their symbol.

Alright, we have come to the end of this chapter and we will be moving on to the next chapter which is the last chapter in this book. There, we will discuss the hidden agenda of this community, our safety amid these people, what we can do as God's children, what our parents can do and what churches can do to stand against the movement of the LGBTQ+ community without causing pain to others.

Don't be tired, darling. We can do this! See you there!

CHAPTER SIX

SOUND OF ALARM!

Of course, each time an alarm rings in your bedroom, it is either to alert you of school time, sleep time or time to do your homework. The sound of the alarm gets you prepared for the task ahead of you. Now let's find out what this alarm is saying concerning LGBTQ+ movements.

Their Agenda

Although the LGBTQ+ community stated their agenda is all about making sure everyone especially their members are treated fairly and equally, no matter who they love or how they feel about themselves.

Yet, there seems to be hidden agenda which is to reduce the population of people across the country and especially Africans. You know, when people of the same gender marry, they can never give birth. The highest they can do is to adopt kids.

Now, here is a critical question we should be asking and the question is,

"Are we safe?"

The answer to the question above depends on how aware we are and the steps we are all taking to stand up against the movement especially knowing their targeted groups.

Who is their target?

The truth is whether you like it or not, the LGBTQ+ movement is spreading very fast and it is gaining ground every day. Now, **their targets are the kids**. As I write, if you should go online, you will see a lot of books written to encourage and lure kids into accepting LGBTQ+. Not just that, they are seriously publishing articles and releasing videos on YouTube that promote LGBTQ+.

In fact, some of the children's school materials are littered with LGBTQ+ content. Recently, I saw a YouTube video where a young parent was reporting that his son (8 years old) saw an LGBTQ+ erotic book in his school library. That's how bad it has become! They know that kids are inquisitive and they are quick to adopt new systems.

What can you do as a kid, parent, and church to stay safe in all of this?

As a kid

Don't feel you're too little to do something, friend. There are lots of things you can do in your own little way to fight against this move.

1. **Awareness**

The very first thing is to be aware and thank God that you are now fully aware. That makes it a lot easier for you. This book has informed you about the LGBTQ+ community and why you shouldn't be part as a child of God.

2. **Talk to Your Parents**

The next thing is that you should never hide anything from your parents. Always talk to your parents about your friends, school activities, and how you feel towards the same gender and the opposite gender. Talk to them about your feelings generally. Talk to them about the books you read and the movies you see.

As a Parent

You have the largest chunk of work to do as a parent. If you fail in your duties over your kids, it will bring in lots of trouble for you and for them too. Now, you are fully aware of the LGBTQ+ movement, its agenda and its target. You are now saddled with the responsibility of ensuring your kid is out of this.

The very first thing you need to do as a parent is to make friends with your kids. Don't be the kind of parent that just goes to work and comes back with plenty of money for the children without spending quality time with them. Eek! Do you think all they need is your money? No! They need your time more than the money.

Be very close to your kids. Be keen to know what they are passing through emotionally. Help them to identify their genders. Never let their friends take over your roles in their lives because it might be disastrous if they do.

Have good listening skills as a parent. Be patient, calm and understanding enough to know what they are going through. Be always ready to help them in the most loving way you can. Take for instance, if your girl child confides in you that she is mostly attracted to fellow girls, you don't have to be mad with her. Simply take her through a process of love and make her see why she can't do such as a child of God.

As much as you can, make your kids feel safer to confide in you than their friends. Also, always go through their school work and materials. Scrutinize the kind of movies or TV shows they see and the kinds of friends they keep. You must be a good observer as a parent. Observe the kind of lifestyles your kids prefer and their behavioural patterns. And be ready to give them good guides where necessary.

Finally, learn to always put your kids through God's words as a Christian parent. Buy Christian materials for your kids and find a good time to discuss them together. Teach them how to talk to God in prayers and how to make the Bible their best companion.

As a Church

Do you know that a lot of churches are in full support of LGBTQ+ movements? Gay and lesbian marriages are being endorsed in some churches. The church is supposed to be a place where worship occurs in truth and holiness but the reverse is the case in these churches.

As a living church, we must be ready to maintain our stand against the movement of LGBTQ+ in our society. From time to time, the church should educate members on LGBTQ+ and what God says about it without promoting hatred.

DISCLAIMER!

This book does not encourage you to pick fights with those who are identified as LGBTQ+ nor does the book permit you to mock them. No! That is not the intent and concept of this book. The book is written to expose our kids to the concept of LGBQT+ so that they are aware before time and to make the right decisions as Christians.

Let's not forget the part of the Bible that says we should pursue peace with all people (Hebrews 12:14) and our Lord Jesus said in Matthew 5:9 that "Blessed are the peacemakers: for they shall be called the children of God". As much as we can, let us be at peace with all men. The Bible never permit us to see others as inferior to us. Treat all men with love and respect.

It is good you know that we are in the era of freedom and you have no right to impose your will on others. Everyone has the right to choose the life they will live. This book is meant to guide you and your family to choose the right part as Christians and not otherwise.

Voila! We have come to the end of an amazing journey. I am super excited we made it this far! Tell me, friend, did you enjoy the ride?

Alright, do not forget all that you have learnt in this book. If there is anything you do not understand, always talk to Mom or Dad about it. Be a good kid, ok?

Once again, it is nice to have you on this amazing journey. Bye!

ABOUT THE AUTHOR

Nwafor Titilola Deborah is a dedicated professional and a woman of many talents. She began her educational journey at the University College Hospital (UCH) in Ibadan, where she earned the prestigious titles of Registered Nurse (RN) and Registered Midwife (RM).

Continuing her quest for knowledge, she pursued her studies at the University of Ibadan (UI), where she achieved both a Bachelor of Education (B.Ed.) and a Master of Education (M.Ed.) in Health Education.

With a strong commitment to her field, Nwafor Titilola Deborah relocated to Port-Harcourt with her family. There, she embarked on an academic journey at the University of Port-Harcourt, where she earned a Master of Science (MSc) degree in Community Health. Her thirst for knowledge led her to Ignatius Ajuru University, where she reached the pinnacle of her academic pursuits by obtaining a Doctor of Philosophy (PhD) degree in Community Health.

Beyond her academic achievements, Nwafor Titilola Deborah is a devoted Christian, known for her talents as a minstrel, worship leader, and songwriter. Her passion for health and wellness has also provided her with opportunities to deliver health talks and guidance at various women's conventions, fellowships, and gatherings, focusing on topics related to women, youths, children, and relationships.

Currently, Nwafor Titilola Deborah serves as an Assistant Director of Nursing at the University of Port-Harcourt Teaching Hospital, where she continues to make a significant impact in the healthcare sector. She shares her life's journey with her beloved husband, Dr. C.E. Nwafor, a renowned cardiologist, and they are blessed with three wonderful children, comprising two boys and one girl.

www.ingramcontent.com/pod-product-compliance
Lightning Source LLC
LaVergne TN
LVHW010506160826
845677LV00012B/2678

* 9 7 8 9 7 8 7 8 2 9 4 5 5 *